Foreword

(The front cover picture was taken Circa 1998.)

A small collection of poems that I have written for my precious mother.

Some of these writings were selected primarily because I was inspired by her. I would like for her to know that her words to me did not fall upon deaf ears. They have remained and continue to echo throughout the chambers of my heart.

I believe that I have lost more writings than I can remember but here are some that I kept. They were written at different points in my life. These pieces of literature do however carry the same feeling. That feeling is, that my mother has always, and I believe, will always have an unconditional love for all her children. Not just me.

Having said that, I will go on to state that I believe that a child can never love the parent as much as the parent loves the child. Especially the mother, who, with the help of God Almighty, gave life.

These are the miracles my God performs.

Mom, I pray to my God that he allows me to take care of you and protect you as you have with me throughout my life.

Table of Contents

ANTES QUE SALGA EL SOL

Alonzo "Spiceman" Acosta
7/30/2002

Antes que salga el sol
Todavía el gallo no canta
En él último cuarto se oye
Mi madre, querida santa

En levantarse tan temprano
Sé que hace un gran esfuerzo
Diciendo "ahorita despertaran
mis hijos y nietos,
Tengo que hacer almuerzo"

Pero así es esa mujer
La quien yo llamo madre
"...hay que ganarle al sol,
antes que se haga tarde"

Toda su vida ha sufrido
Tanto que ha trabajado
Siempre pidiéndole a su
Diosito
"...no te vayas de mi lado"

Siempre fue mi maestra,
Mi guía, mi mejor amiga
Orando constante a su Dios
Que sus hijos les bendiga
"...bendice mis hijos, Dios mío,

No los dejes llegar en mal.
Pues soy una sola y pobre
madre
Pero te pido sin igual."

Esto yo lo digo por experiencia
Desde joven yo fui su testigo
Viendo que por mí todo lo
sacrificaba
Y por eso sigo el camino que
yo sigo

Hoy venimos a saludarla
Con ella vamos a celebrar
Venimos a comer y gozar
Decir cuentos y cantar

"Que viva mi madre querida
Hay abuelita tan preciosa"
Pasamos todos a besarla
Y entregarle una rosa

Que tenga un Feliz día
Querida Madre Mía.
Y hoy pedimos todos
Que Dios nos la bendiga

EN TUS MANOS

Alonzo "Spiceman" Acosta
6-27-06

Como una flor
Que nace en el desierto
Porque es Tierna y frágil
Fracasar le queda cierto

¿Pero realmente piensas que
sí?
Piensas que el sol tan fuerte
Hará caer esta florecita
¿Que solo se espera su muerte?

Piensas que su piel
Tan bella y suave al sentir
Se secará con el calor
¿Y el desierto la hace morir?

Pues yo pienso que no
Aunque la miren débil al
comenzar
Ella ha puesto una meta
Y en su mente solo hay que
ganar

Si yo fuera hombre
Que a puesta dinero
Pondría mi fe y dinero en ella
Con seguridad de llegar primero

Porque ella es una madre con
hijos
Y su meta es sacarlos adelante

Ella levanta su rostro firme
Hay bella, tan elegante
Aunque el desierto es duro
Y muchas veces se desea el
morir
Es más grande el amor de sus
hijos
Y ese amor la deja más que
sobrevivir

Dios mío, en Ti descansa mi fe
Hoy pongo mi vida en Tus
manos
Este día por mí y mis hijos te
pido
Haz mis caminos derechos y
sanos

Deja que a donde llegue
Llegues Tu primero
Porque Tú eres mi guía y amigo
Tu eres mi consejero

Deja llegar que algún día
recuerde
Aquel tiempo que fue hay tan
duro
Y que se diga "ella tuvo fe en su
Dios
Eso si es por seguro.

" Hay Dios mío,
Hoy pongo mi vida en Tus manos"

Mom, a few years ago. Wooooohoooo!!!

MADRE MIA

Alonzo "Spiceman" Acosta
12/1994

Doy gracias a mi Dios por usted.
Por los buenos consejos que siempre me da.
No nomás a mí,

pero a mis hermanos también!

Doy Gracias a mi Dios por usted.

Por todos los sacrificios que siempre hace

para que sus hijos estén con bien,

...Aunque usted no!

Doy gracias a mi Dios por usted.

Porque cuando no encontré

quien tuviera fe en mí,

¡Usted y Dios sí!

Doy gracias a mi Dios por usted.

Y pido que yo llegué a ser un buen padre

Como usted es una buena madre conmigo

Madre Mia

Doy gracias a mi Dios por usted.

MY PRAYER FOR TODAY

Alonzo "Spiceman" Acosta
10/12/2003 10:36 AM

Human endurance is what has allowed humans to survive even the very own destruction of themselves. It is to that endurance that I submit my life, for that endurance is my faith in my God. It is with this endurance and faith that I go forth in the morning and lay myself to rest in the evening.

There was a time in my life when I felt I had no hope. I prayed to my God for help. I asked my God, **"Lord send some body to show me the way for I am lost."** And My God the Lord did send somebody to show me the way, but I was full of pride and decided not to accept this help. I did not know how to accept help. It took many years as well as trials and tribulations before I was able to see the true facts and how I am the only one who can help myself. Only I can let peace rest in my heart, a place where anger and hate must and will not live.

I continue to ask my God to let me be like my Mother. For she is a humble faithful servant of God. I asked my God then, and I continue to ask my God to this day for the strength, courage, and endurance to continue to live my life as if this day is the first and last day of my life.

I ask my God to allow me to teach by learning. I ask my God to allow me to love by giving love. I ask my God

to allow me to be remembered by remembering those who need remembering. I ask my God to allow me to

live by acknowledging death. Just as the sun rises with a smile, I pray that I might have the peace of heart to

smile as it sets in the evening. For then I will know that I have made a fine day out of a truly fine day that was given to me by my God.

There are those out there who still suffer and know that they do. They do not however know how to accept any help that is sent by my God to them. I pray oh Lord that you open their minds and hearts so that they can see and accept this help that is commonly called opportunity or chance. For I have often stated that *"Chance encounters are not by chance but by God."* I pray, oh Lord that you bring down these walls that have been built out of fear to protect themselves but only serves to do more harm than help. These walls, that, while they might protect, also serve to suffocate the very life that they seek and pray for.

This is my prayer Lord, not only for me, but for those who are now in the same midst of suffering as I have been. I pray for those who know they want and need help but know not how to receive and accept it. Oh, Lord open their hearts and minds for they need to start to live a life of happiness and gratefulness. This, my Lord, is my prayer today... and everyday... for them and for me.

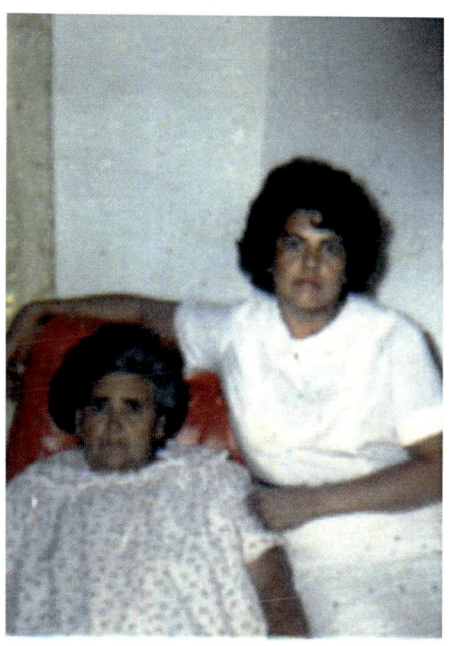

Mom and Grandma Rosa.

My boys and me
They spent their summers with mom
since they were toddlers!!

SANDIA

Alonzo "Spiceman" Acosta
04/08/2002

Mama, mama mira lo que papi compro
Un Sandia, Sandia, papi compro sandia
Espérense hijos al rato la partimos
Primero en el helero para que se en fríe

Hay mi viejo de donde trajiste esta sandia
Mírala vieja, esta tan bonita y tan grande
Hay para todos mis hijos y luego queda
Anda, ve, invita tu comadre Cande

De qué color será, rojo o amarilla
Ha de estar tan sabrosa
Que rico comer después de cena
En esta tarde tan calorosa

Si fue un buen precio
El vendedor de la esquina me conoce
Le pregunte cuanto por la sandía, compadre
Me dijo, las doy en quince, pero a ti en doce

Hay mi viejo tan querido
Siempre buscas como orar un peso
Por eso siempre digo que eres el mejor padre
Ven pronto para darte un beso

Pues si por eso la compre vieja
¿Tú crees que fue para orar un peso?
No, no mi querida vieja
La compre porque quería un beso

Aye que sabrosa esta Sandia...
Y los besos también

THE MARBLES
By Alonzo M Acosta
5/7/2003 8:26:06 AM

It seems that lately I spend more and more time with my mother. The strange part is that the more time I spend listening to her instead of having her listen to me. I find that I am discovering a totally different person. Yes, my mother is a totally different person.

After 21 years of being away, I moved back to my hometown. For several reasons, but the main reason is that my mother was involved in a car wreck. This brought me here from there in a heartbeat. I saw mother not doing well and decided to stay an extra week to make sure she was ok. That was 3 years ago.

Well as time would have it and I am sure my Great God had plenty to do with it, I came from where I left, only to find the tranquility of my hometown and my home, and of course my mother. (interruption mom was calling me, lost track of thought)

I found myself in a small town with nothing to do but take care of a wonderful woman who needed me almost as much as I needed her when I was young. No, I believe that I am wrong. I have always and will always need her more than she needs me. But I will add that now that I myself am a parent, believe that she will always love me more than I love her for I find that the love that I have for my children is unequaled in any aspect what so ever.

One day as we were driving to her doctor appointment which is 76 miles away, she started to tell me one of her "when I was young" stories. I don't know how we got into the subject of marbles, but she got a big smile on her face as she started down memory lane to bring back a time of her youth. "Your Uncle Felipe always had marbles. He had coffee cans full of marbles, cat's eyes, little clear one, swirlies, big steel ball bearing ones, tolonches as they were called... well he just had hundreds of marbles in coffee cans." She said all in one breath.

"I was just a young kid then and some of the neighborhood boys talked me into going and stealing some of your Uncle Felipe's tolonches to go play marbles with. They told me that if I had these big tolonches then I was sure to win. So being a naive little girl I went and got some of my uncle's tolonches, and sure enough it wasn't long before they took advantage of me and won them all from me. I went home crying."

"What did you do?" I asked, rather agitated at those stupid kids who took my mom's tolonches.

"Well when your uncle came home and found his marbles scattered and yelled out to me, 'negra, did you get some of my tolonches?' I started to cry, and I guess I didn't know how to lie so I told him what happened. He calmed down and he told me that it was just a trick by those boys to steal the tolonches." She said.

She said, "you know I even saw one of them at a funeral the other day, and I was going to ask him if he remembered when he took my marbles." With a sweet smile on her face she asked me, "Can you imagine after all these years I still want my marbles back?"

Well, I was a little upset and told my ma, "Hey ma, where is this guy, I will go get your marbles back, I don't care where he is."

"oh, si, do you think that he still had those marbles? Besides mijo, he is an old man by now and you will not disrespect him." She told me in a very firm motherly voice.

"Ok, ma but I am sure that between the two of us we can take that guy." I stated in a chuckle.

Well we got to the doctor's office and we left our conversation there, but now that I am remembering my mother a few days before Mother's Day, I have come to see that she had a life before she was my mother. Why, she was even a little girl who got cheated out of marbles.

I think that for this Mother's Day, I will give her a bucket full of marbles, and on the top of the bucket a brand-new bag of Tolonches.

All of us!

Jamming at mom's

Just kicking back during Christmas

UNFINISHED BUSINESS

Alonzo "SPICEMAN" Acosta
10-1993

TONIGHT, I FIND MYSELF
IN THE MIDST OF MY SOLITUDE,
TAKING INTO ACCOUNT
ALL THE ACTIONS OF WHICH I AM CHIEF.

IT IS OFT THAT I REMINISE
THE TENDER MOMENTS
AND THE BRUTAL DAYS
ALL OF WHICH COMPOSE
WHO I NOW AM

AS I TALLY THIS LEDGER
THAT I DARE CALL MY LIFE...
I AM ENCOUNTERED IN
UNFINISHED BUSINESS...

Negocios Sin Terminar

Alonzo "SPICEMAN" Acosta
1-1994

Esta noche me encuentro
En medio de mi soledad
Tomando en cuenta
Todos los hechos de cuales yo soy Rey

Siempre recuerdo
Los tiernos momentos
Y días difíciles
Lo cual todo encierra
Lo que hoy soy

Y cuando escucho esto,
Esto que llamo mi Vida
Siempre me encuentro involucrado...
En Asuntos Sin Terminar...

(I translated Unfinished Business, into Spanish
because I really connect with it)

VALIENT SIRE

Alonzo "SPICEMAN" Acosta
CIRCA 1986

BE COURAGEOUS YOUNG VALIANT SIRE
FOR COURAGE IS NOT THE FRUIT A FOOL BARES,
WHEN GLOOM IS AT IT'S PEAK,
WHEN NIGHT GETS DARK NO MORE;
ON BOTTOM THERE IS NO MORE LOW

ONLY ONE THING LEFT FOR YOU TO DO
YOUR HEAD DO HOLD UP HIGH!
WITH COURAGE AND TRUST TO YOUR RIGHT
WITH HOPE AND PEACE TO YOUR LEFT
FORGET NOT WHAT YOU WERE BEFORE
FOR THAT, IS THE FIRE ON YOUR MARCH FORWARD
... AND FORWARD YOU SHALL GO!

SO ONCE AGAIN I URGE...

BE COURAGEOUS YOUNG VALIANT SIRE
FOR COURAGE IS NOT THE FRUIT A FOOL BEARS
LIFE EACH DAY HARD, BUT IN KINDNESS
LIFE IT FULL, AND WITH RESPECT
FOR YOU DO NOT KNOW YOUR DESTINY
NOR WHEN YOUR JOURNEY WILL END
JUST ASSURANCE THAT IT WILL END.

I WRITE

Alonzo "SPICEMAN" Acosta
Circa 1993

I am Jose Alonzo Melendez Hernandez Medina De Acosta. There are five of us in my family (brothers & sisters). I am father of a daughter and two wonderful boys whom I love and care for very much.

I am a Christian by choice, for life (I pray!)
I humbly try to do the Lord's work.

I am a writer, I write…
That's all… I just write.
It comes as a natural to me.

I am a zodiac Gemini, supposedly I am two personalities, I agree.
One part of me enjoys the private life to which I have allowed myself to become accustomed to. The other part enjoys the public life, to be and work on center stage. I do however reserve my right to retire to my private world where I am at liberty to write or curl up to a good book.

I am an early riser, yet I love to stay up late at night, which makes it very hard on this human body of mine.

I try to be the friend who will give you the shirt off his back. Yet I feel I need to save for a rainy day, (not that I do.)

I try to live sincere and honest. Not just because God demands it of me, but because I am by nature that way.

I believe in an honest day's pay for and honest day's work… fair is fair!

I have been a musician all my life.
Music runs through my veins.
I am single, I enjoy my solitude.
I also enjoy being able to smile with someone special.

I work 12-17 hours a day.
Not so much to gain a multitude of material things but to be able to provide for my family.

I am an avid learner, I love the knowledge, knowledge brings.
I enjoy listening... to a good gospel preacher, to a good song, to the wails
of a hurting friend, to the early morning songbird, to the melancholic cry of
the evening cricket, and to you talk about whatever you have to say.

I believe that wise counsel listens.

I hate hate. I hate prejudice.
I hate hypocrisy. I hate charlatans.

I love my children. I love life within itself.

I am, at this time thinking of you.
I hope that you are thinking of me.
I am happy that our paths have crossed, even if it just for a while.
I smile because they did cross.

I am on a quest, which shall take the rest of my life, yet I am hopeful that
this life-long endeavor will lead me to Jesus in heaven.

I have in my mind a closet full of true-life stories and adventures, most of
which I write in my private book. I leave this book to my children, for that
matter, all my writings belong to my children except...
The one written for you, someday (with your help) I will finish it.

I am called Spiceman for my words.
I hope to be called Christian for my actions.

This is who I think that I am. Whether you accept me or not...
I remain me!

I thank God for your existence.

Sincerely,

Alonzo "Spiceman" Acosta

Ay Señor

Alonzo "SPICEMAN" Acosta
12-99

Ay Señor
mírame come me encuentro
pero para que te cuento
si tú ya lo sabes

en oración
de rodias yo te pido
perdóname
y ayuda tú pobre hijo

mándame
un ángel que me aconseje
porque ya
estoy cansado de este tipo de vida

recuerdo aquel
aquel ayer cuando era feliz
tanto amor
tanto que yo amaba

espero que
que me concedes lo que te pido
y si me dices que no Señor
suficiente fue......
suficiente fue que me hayas oído

ay~~~~~~~~~~~ Señor

ESTA CANCION

ALONZO "SPICEMAN" ACOSTA
June 1988

Esta canción,
Con llanto en mis ojos,
Y orgullo,
Dedico a mi madre

Porque sus oraciones
Muchas que fueron
Llegaron a los cielos
Con mi Diosito

El día que yo nací
Mi Dios me dio el orgullo
De ser hijo suyo
Querida Madrecita

Porque mi Dios bien lo sabia
Que yo ocuparía
Un gran amor
Como el que usted me ha
dado

{Bridge}
Y hoy,
Por ser día de su Santo
He venido a cantarle
Lo mucho que la amo

Usted conmigo ahí estuvo
Cuando más la necesitaba
Pidiéndole a mi Diosito

Y hoy,
Madre, madrecita
Quisiera yo decirle
Cuanto yo la amo

Le doy gracias a mi Dios
Porque me la ha guardo
Todos estos anos

Yo se
que usted paso
Muchas Noches sin dormir
Esperando que yo llegara

Mirando por la ventana
Cada carro que pasaba
Suspirando y orando
Hasta que yo llegara

{Bridge}

Quisiera yo tener la fuerza
Para amar yo a mis hijos
Como usted me ha amado

{SLOW}
Querida madrecita

Buscando Clemencia

Alonzo "SPICEMAN" Acosta
12-1999

Que truenen los truenos
Que caigan los rayos
Que lleguen las lluvias
Yo siempre te adoro

Puras tribulaciones
Ya no hallo la puerta
Tú te me escondes
Me siento tan solo

Yo sé que he pecado
Igual me arrepiento
sin ti no ay vida
Yo lo reconozco

Los días oscuros
Las noches iguales
Satán me rodea
Me siento tan débil

(1st bridge)

(2nd bridge)

*Pero siempre invoco tu
nombre
Se que tardas, tu no olvidas
Te pido,
mis ojos llenos de llanto
Señor…. No te olvides de mi*

*Quiero entrar a tu reino
Quiero tener vida eterna
Se que eres el camino
Tengo tiempo perdido*

Con fe yo te ruego
Hincado, humillado
Buscando clemencia
No encuentro tu rostro

Pero siempre invoco tu
nombre
*Se que tardas, tu no olvidas
Te pido, mis ojos llenos de
llanto*
Señor…. No te olvides de mi
Señor…. No te olvides de mi
Señor…. No te olvides de mi

Los Hechos

Alonzo "Spiceman" Acosta
11-20-02

al ver que el tiempo me alcanza
cuando en el espejo miro mis canas
al ver mis hijos crecer a adultos
y que a la vida le echan ganas

cuando por teléfono hablo con mis hermanos
los que se encuentran lejos de mi
recuerdo los tiempos de mi juventud
y deseo que ellos estuvieran aquí

(written 1-11-07)

luego escucho las palabras de mi madre
que se encuentran gravadas en mi corazón
dichos verdaderos y profundos
y digo "mama tenía mucha razón"

hoy si entiendo lo de nuestra vida
que es algo bello de naturaleza
así como amanece fuerte el sol
y luego sienta tranquillo, pero sin fuerza
y ver sentar el sol, así es la vida
conocida solamente por los hechos
los hijos se ponen a recordar y llorar
pues eso son sus dados derechos

ya de grande recuerdo a mi padre
el cual entiendo que no fue perfecto
pero reconozco que el sí me amaba
y en mis ojos eso lo hace recto

espero que también mis hijos
pueden ver lo mucho que yo los amo
y doy mi vida por ellos
ojalá que no lo tomen por en vano

porque al final son los hechos
lo que determinan de una vida, el valor
llena de amor y serenidad
vivida con todo vigor

Al final, son los hechos...

Mom's sayings

Here are some of mom's favorite sayings.

"hhhuuuhh!!!"

This can mean anything she wants it to mean. From disapproval to "I told you so". It can mean anything.

¡Come Monda!!

This means you are not getting anything; or eat... well actually I have never been able to find out what **Monda** is!

¡Cállate la lengua!

This means she is happy but shut up anyway!! ☺

¡Dime con quien andas y te digo quién eres!

This means you are who you hang around with!!

¡Mira Alonzo, No me hagas blasfemar!!

She tells me this when I am kidding around with her and she wants me to leave her alone. Ha ha ha ha ha